The Beauty of God's Creation

(In the Midst of Corruption)

Dr John G Leslie

Deluge Press

ISBN-13: 978-0692714829 (Deluge Press)
ISBN-10: 0692714820

Deluge Press
Gallup, New Mexico

DEDICATION

To my wife Barbara,
mother of our children and
my soul mate for over 35 years.
My children Peter, Anna and Teresa.
Also Nancy, Jennifer and Greg my siblings,
who all appreciate the beauty of God's Creation.
Finally, to my parents, who taught me to love God and
the wonders of His Creation.

CONTENTS

Acknowledgments vi

Introduction 1

The Creation… 2

Humans with Words of Faith 6

Reptiles/Amphibians 8

Fish & Aquatic Life 10

Birds 12

Mammals 14

Insects & Flowers 16

Insects 20

Trees 32

Mountains & Valleys 36

Fossils 46

Clouds 50

Geometric Design 52

Conclusion 54

The Creator's Plan for You 55

About the author 56

Acknowledgments

Several online sources have been accessed regarding information of some of the pictures and their composition. Included are Wikipedia, and others that are listed in each footnote in which they appear with their permission to reproduce. Also used was Nelson's "The New Strong's Exhaustive Concordance of the Bible", J. Strong, Thomas Nelson Publisher, Nashville TN. 1966. Thank you to Chuck Scott, C & E Rock Sales, for the well polished petrified wood sections. Most photographs are done by myself. All rights are retained, except for use in non-profit publications with acknowledgement to John G. Leslie.

To God Be The Glory

Introduction

Photography is such a vehicle to express ideas and concepts! It is plain to me that the earth and life on it has beauty and also something harsh and terrifying at times. How does one reconcile these diverse aspects of the earth and natural life? So many nature programs try to make the gory details of a lion tearing a wildebeest apart as some normal part of "Nature, Red in Tooth and Claw."

Yet, in contrast, I accept the teaching of the Bible:

Romans 8:18 Yet what we suffer now is nothing compared to the glory he will reveal to us later. **19** For all creation is waiting eagerly for that future day when God will reveal who his children really are. **20 Against its will, all creation was subjected to God's curse. But with eager hope, 21 the creation looks forward to the day when it will join God's children in glorious freedom from death and decay. 22 For we know that all creation has been groaning as in the pains of childbirth right up to the present time. 23** And we believers also groan, even though we have the Holy Spirit within us as a foretaste of future glory, for we long for our bodies to be released from sin and suffering. We, too, wait with eager hope for the day when God will give us our full rights as his adopted children, including the new bodies he has promised us. **24** We were given this hope when we were saved. (If we already have something, we don't need to hope for it. **25** But if we look forward to something we don't yet have, we must wait patiently and confidently.)

Isaiah 65:17 Look! **I am creating new heavens and a new earth**, and no one will even think about the old ones anymore.

2 Peter 3: 11 Since everything around us is going to be destroyed like this, what holy and godly lives you should live, **12** looking forward to the day of God and hurrying it along. On that day, he will set the heavens on fire, and the elements will melt away in the flames. **13** But we are looking forward to the new heavens and new earth he has promised, a world filled with God's righteousness. **14** And so, dear friends, while you are waiting for these things to happen, make every effort to be found living peaceful lives that are pure and blameless in his sight.

Then why do this book? Because the glory of God shows in glimmers even now through the fallen creation, so as to give us hope to turn to Him in repentance and obedience to the saving of our souls/spirits to eternal life.

The Creation: Made Good

Genesis 1:1 In the beginning God created the heavens and the earth. 2 The **earth was formless and empty**, and darkness covered the deep waters. And the Spirit of God was hovering over the surface of the waters. **3** Then God said, "**Let there be light**," and there was light. **4** And God saw that the light was good. Then he **separated the light from the darkness**. **5** God called the **light "day"** and the **darkness "night."** And **evening passed and morning came, marking the FIRST DAY.**

6 Then God said, "Let there be a **space between the waters, to separate the waters of the heavens from the waters of the earth."** **7** And that is what happened. God made this space to separate the waters of the earth from the waters of the heavens. **8** God called the **space "sky."** And evening passed and morning came, marking the **SECOND DAY**.

9Then God said, "Let the waters **beneath the sky flow together into one place, so dry ground may appear**." And that is what happened. **10** God called the **dry ground "land"** and the **waters "seas."** And God saw that it was good. **11** Then God said, "Let the **land sprout with vegetation**—every sort of seed-bearing plant, and trees that grow seed-bearing fruit. **These seeds will then produce the kinds** of plants and trees from which they came." And that is what happened. **12** The land produced **vegetation**—all sorts of seed-bearing **plants**, and **trees** with seed-bearing fruit. Their seeds produced plants and trees of the same kind. And God saw that **it was good**. **13** And evening passed and morning came, marking the **THIRD DAY.**

14 Then God said, "Let **lights appear in the sky to separate the day from the night**. Let them be **signs** to mark the **seasons, days, and years**. **15** Let these **lights in the sky shine down on the earth**." And that is what happened. **16** God made **two great lights**—the larger one to **govern the day**, and the smaller one to **govern the night**. He also made the **stars**. **17** God set these lights in the sky to light the earth, **18** to govern the day and night, and to separate the light from the darkness. And God saw that **it was good**. **19** And evening passed and morning came, marking the **FOURTH DAY.**

20 Then God said, "**Let the waters swarm with fish and other life. Let the skies be filled with birds of every kind."** **21** So God created **great sea creatures** and **every living thing that scurries and swarms in the water**, and **every sort of bird**—each producing offspring of the same kind. And God saw that **it was good**. **22** Then God blessed them, saying, "**Be fruitful and multiply**. Let the fish **fill the seas**, and let the birds **multiply on the earth**." **23** And evening passed and morning came, marking the **FIFTH DAY.**

24 Then God said, "Let the **earth produce every sort of animal, each producing offspring of the same kind—livestock, small animals that scurry along the ground, and wild animals**." And that is what happened. **25** God made all sorts of wild animals, livestock, and small animals, each able to produce offspring of the same kind. And God saw that it was good.

26 Then God said, "Let us **make human beings in our image**, to be like us. **They will reign over the fish in the sea, the birds in the sky, the livestock, all the wild animals on the earth, and the small animals that scurry along the ground**."

27 So God created human beings in his own image. In the image of God he created them; **male and female** he created them.

28 Then God blessed them and said, "**Be fruitful and multiply. Fill the earth and govern it. Reign over the fish in the sea, the birds in the sky, and all the animals that scurry along the ground.**" **29** Then God said, "Look! I have given you every seed-bearing plant throughout the earth and all the fruit trees for your food. **30** And I have given every green plant as food for all the wild animals, the birds in the sky, and the small animals that scurry along the ground—everything that has life." And that is what happened. **31** Then God looked over all he had made, and he saw that **it was very good**! And evening passed and morning came, marking the **SIXTH DAY**.

Genesis 2:1 So the creation of the heavens and the earth and everything in them was completed. **2** On the seventh day God had finished his work of creation, so he rested from all his work. **3** And God blessed the **SEVENTH DAY** and declared it holy, because it was the day when he rested from all his work of creation.

Then Came the Fall, Corruption of Man, the Flood, and All Things Became Corrupted

(Yet, there remains to this day, semblances of God's beauty in the Creation post-Flood.)

Genesis 6: 5 The LORD observed **the extent of human wickedness on the earth**, and he saw that everything they thought or imagined was consistently and totally evil. **6** So **the LORD was sorry he had ever made them and put them on the earth. It broke his heart. 7** And the LORD said, "**I will wipe this human race I have created from the face of the earth. Yes, and I will destroy every living thing—all the people, the large animals, the small animals that scurry along the ground, and even the birds of the sky**. I am sorry I ever made them." **8 But Noah found favor with the LORD.**

Genesis 7:15 Two by two they came into the boat, representing every living thing that breathes. … **18** As the waters rose higher and higher above the ground, the boat floated safely on the surface. … **23 God wiped out every living thing on the earth—people, livestock, small animals that scurry along the ground, and the birds of the sky. All were destroyed. The only people who survived were Noah and those with him in the boat.**

Genesis 9: 8 Then God told Noah and his sons, **9** "**I hereby confirm my covenant with you and your descendants**, **10** and **with all the animals that were on the boat with you—the birds, the livestock, and all the wild animals—every living creature on earth**. 11 Yes**, I am confirming my covenant with you.** Never again will floodwaters kill all living creatures; **never again will a flood destroy the earth.**" **12** Then God said, "I am giving you a **sign of my covenant** with you and with all living creatures, for all generations to come. **13** I have placed **my rainbow in the clouds**. It is the sign of my covenant with you and with all the earth. **14** When I send clouds over the earth, the rainbow will appear in the clouds, **15** and **I will remember my covenant with you and with all living creatures. Never again will the floodwaters destroy all life**. **16**When I see the rainbow in the clouds, I will remember the eternal covenant between God and every living creature on earth." **17** Then God said to Noah, "Yes, this rainbow is the sign of the covenant I am confirming with all the creatures on earth."

Man Made in God's Image

Genesis 1:26 Then God said, "Let us make human beings in our image, to be like us. They will reign over the fish in the sea, the birds in the sky, the livestock, all the wild animals on the earth, and the small animals that scurry along the ground." **27** So God created human beings in his own image. In the image of God he created them; male and female he created them.

Man Made To Worship God

John 4:21 Jesus replied, "Believe me, dear woman, the time is coming when it will no longer matter whether you worship the Father on this mountain or in Jerusalem. **22**You Samaritans know very little about the one you worship, while we Jews know all about him, for salvation comes through the Jews. **23** But the time is coming—indeed it's here now—when true worshipers will worship the Father in spirit and in truth. The Father is looking for those who will worship him that way. **24** For God is Spirit, so those who worship him must worship in spirit and in truth." **25** The woman said, "I know the Messiah is coming—the one who is called Christ. When he comes, he will explain everything to us." **26** Then Jesus told her, "I AM the Messiah!"

Man Corrupted By Sin

Genesis 3:17 And to the man he said, "Since you listened to your wife and ate from the tree whose fruit I commanded you not to eat, the ground is cursed because of you. All your life you will struggle to scratch a living from it. … **22** Then the LORD God said, "Look, the human beings have become like us, knowing both good and evil. What if they reach out, take fruit from the tree of life, and eat it? Then they will live forever!" **23** So the LORD God banished them from the Garden of Eden, and he sent Adam out to cultivate the ground from which he had been made.

Man Redeemed (Creation To Take On Incorruption)

Romans 8: 20 Against its will, all creation was subjected to God's curse. But with eager hope, **21** the creation looks forward to the day when it will join God's children in glorious freedom from death and decay.

John 3:16 "For this is how God loved the world: He gave his one and only Son, so that everyone who believes in him will not perish but have eternal life.

Galatians 3: 13 But Christ has rescued us from the curse pronounced by the law. When he was hung on the cross, he took upon himself the curse for our wrongdoing. For it is written in the Scriptures, "Cursed is everyone who is hung on a tree." **14 Through Christ Jesus, God has blessed the Gentiles with the same blessing he promised to Abraham, so that we who are believers might receive the promised Holy Spirit through faith.**

Humans with Words of Faith: a Musician, Social Reformer, Political Leader, and Scientist

Johann Sebastian Bach (upper right) "widely regarded as the greatest of all composers of music for Christian worship, was born in 1685 in Eisenach, Thuringia, Germany, into a family of distinguished musicians. In 1708, shortly after marrying Maria Barbara Bach, he became court organist to the Duke of Weimar, where he wrote his principal compositions for the organ…Bach said, 'Music's only purpose should be the glory of God and the recreation of the human spirit.'" [1]

William Wilberforce (lower left) "(24 August 1759 – 29 July 1833) was an English politician, philanthropist, and a leader of the movement to abolish the slave trade…In 1785, he became an Evangelical Christian, which resulted in major changes to his lifestyle and a lifelong concern for reform…He headed the parliamentary campaign against the British slave trade for twenty years until the passage of the Slave Trade Act of 1807…Milner accompanied Wilberforce to England, and on the journey they read *The Rise and Progress of Religion in the Soul* by Philip Doddridge, a leading early 18th-century English nonconformist… Wilberforce's conversion led him to question whether he should remain in public life. Wilberforce sought guidance from John Newton, a leading Evangelical Anglican clergyman of the day and Rector of St Mary Woolnoth in the City of London. Both Newton and Pitt counseled Wilberforce to remain in politics, and he resolved to do so 'with increased diligence and conscientiousness' as political views were informed by his faith and by his desire to promote Christianity and Christian ethics in private and public life." [2]

Ronald Reagan (lower right) "Kengor's sweeping examination of the spiritual quest of the man he calls a 'practical Christian' should quiet the controversy about whether Reagan had an entrenched faith. Reagan's faith was not only sincere and vocalized throughout his life, Kengor asserts, it also provided fuel for the fire of his single-minded determination to bring down communism." Also, "Without God, there is no virtue because there's no prompting of the conscience. And without God, democracy will not and cannot long endure. If we ever forget that we're one nation under God, then we will be a nation gone under."[3]

Johannes Kepler (upper left) "Those laws [of nature] are within the grasp of the human mind; God wanted us to recognize them by creating us after his own image so that we could share in his own thoughts."Also, "I wanted to become a theologian; for a long time I was unhappy. Now, behold, God is praised by my work even in astronomy." [4]

---

[1] http://www.christians.com/inspirational/jsbach_for_the_glory_of_god.Photo public domain.

[2] https://en.wikipedia.org/wiki/William_Wilberforce. Photo public domain.

[3] http://www.christianitytoday.com/ct/2004/august/10.57.html, and www.christianquotes.info/quotes -by-author/ronald-reagan. photo pub. dom.

[4] http://todayinsci.com/K/Kepler_Johannes/KeplerJohannes-Quotations.htm. photo public domain.

Humans: Examples of Worshipers of God

Reptiles/Amphibians:
Things that Creep Upon the Earth

Genesis 1: 24 And God said, "Let the earth bring forth the living creature after his kind, cattle, and creeping thing, and beast of the earth after his kind: and it was so. **25** And God made the beast of the earth after his kind, and cattle after their kind, and everything that creepeth upon the earth **after his kind**: and **God saw that it was good**. KJV

Yet, now:

Romans 8:22 For we know that **all creation has been groaning as in the pains of childbirth** right up to the present time.

Collared Lizard (*Crotaphytus collaris*: upper left): "They can run on their hind legs, and live mostly in the Southwest deserts of the US. They eat grasshoppers, insects, and other lizards including their own kind. Other lizards, coyotes, roadrunners, and cats will eat them as well." [5]

Desert Tortoise (*Gopherus agassisii*: upper right): "They inhabit desert regions of the Southwest US. To escape heat they burrow and can go without food or water for extended times by concentrating their urine. They are herbivores, only eating plants. Other animals eat them, especially the young when they are still soft shelled. Foxes, Gila monsters, road runners and coyotes are known to feed on them. This tortoise can live up to 35-40 years." [6]

Bull Snake (*Pituophis catenifer sayi*: mid-right): "Is a non-venomous snake that kills its prey by constriction or swallowing it whole. It is found in grassy prairies from Canada to Mexico to Illinois and California. It grows up to 4-6 feet and lives up to 12-25 years. It eats rodents, lizards and frogs, rabbits, and birds if it is nesting on the ground." [7]

Desert Toad (*Bufo alvarius*: lower right) "This toad grows to a large size up to 7 inches, has a smooth skin except for large parotid glands which contain potent toxins that can kill a dog if it picks up the toad. It is found in the Southwest US and Mexico, mostly in areas with scrubs, and desert woodlands. It procreates during the rainy season by laying eggs in small temporary puddles of water. It eats beetles and sometimes other toads. It is nocturnal. This toad can live 10-20 years." [8]

Horned Lizard (Horned Toads or *Phrynosoma platyrhinos: lower left)* "These lizards are found in the western deserts and mountains of US and Mexico. They are vigorous consumers of ants and other ground crawling insects. Yet, insects in swarms can kill them. Other reptiles like snakes have difficulty eating them because of the horny skin. They hibernate in the winter by burying in the sand. When out in the warm sun will flatten themselves to receive heat. Life expectancy is 5-8 years." [9]

[5] https://www.desertmuseum.org/kids/oz/long-fact-sheets/Collared%20Lizard.php

[6] https://www.desertmuseum.org/kids/oz/long-fact-sheets/Desert%20Tortoise.php

[7] http://snake-facts.weebly.com/bullsnake.html

[8] https://www.desertmuseum.org/books/nhsd_desert_toad.php

[9] http://www.desertusa.com/reptiles/horned-lizard.html

Reptiles/Amphibians: Great Diversity With Many Kinds

Fish and Other Diverse Aquatic Life

Genesis 1:20 Then God said, "**Let the waters swarm with fish and other life**…"

Brook trout (*Salvelinus fontinalis* upper left) "is a species of freshwater fish in the salmon family Salmonidae. It is native to Eastern North America in the United States and Canada…Typical lengths of the brook trout vary from 25 to 65 cm (9.8 to 25.6 in), and weights from 0.3 to 3 kg (0.66 to 6.61 lb)." [10]

Jellyfish or **jellies** (upper right) are "major non-polyp form of individuals of the phylum *Cnidaria*. They are typified as free-swimming marine animals consisting of a gelatinous umbrella-shaped bell and trailing tentacles. The bell can pulsate for locomotion, while stinging tentacles can be used to capture prey…As jellyfish are not true fish (which are vertebrates, unlike jellyfish), called jellies…Most jellyfish do not have specialized digestive, osmoregulatory, central nervous, respiratory, or circulatory systems." [11]

Stingray (*Dasyatidae* middle right*)* "Is a fish that can grow 2-4 ft. wide with a tail twice as long. They are found in tropical waters in the western Atlantic Ocean and the Caribbean Sea. They eat shellfish, crabs, shrimp etc. Sharks and other larger fish eat them. The tail can excrete a toxin injected through barbed stingers. Occasional fatal stings have occurred." [12]

Porcupine fish (*Diodontidae Tetraodontiformes* lower right) "A fish that live in tropical seas." They defend themselves by 3 mechanisms: (1) by inflating their bodies, (2) spines that stick out when inflated, and (3) a Tetrodotoxin (neurotoxin) within that is "at least 1200 times more potent than cyanide. Apparently it comes from bacteria that the fish eats. They eat algae and small invertebrates, and are eaten by sharks and Killer whales, with younger ones eaten by dolphins and tuna fish." [13]

Moray eels or **Muraenidae** (lower left) "are a family of cosmopolitan eels. The approximately 200 species in 15 genera are almost exclusively marine, but several species are regularly seen in brackish water, and a few, for example the freshwater moray (*Gymnothorax polyuranodon*), can sometimes be found in fresh water." Morays range in size from 4.5 inches (*Anarchias leucurus*), to 13 ft. (*Strophidon sathete*). [14]

Sharks (middle left) "There are more than 465 known species of sharks living in our oceans today… They have a cartilaginous structure rather calcified bones, breathe through gills (where water has to continuously flow across the gill surface to maintain oxygenation)… eat things like fish, crustaceans, mollusks, plankton, krill, marine mammals and other sharks." They have acutely sensitive smell,[15] and are another group of **Living Fossils** with fossil teeth found in Ordovician strata (450 myo by secular reasoning).[16] Again, so-called "Living Fossils" argue strongly against evolution and long ages for the earth.

---

[10] https://en.wikipedia.org/wiki/Brook_trout
[11] http://en.wikipedia.org/jellyfish/
[12] http://www.stlzoo.org/visit/thingstoseeanddo/stingraysatcaribbeancove/southernstingrayfacts/
[13] https://en.wikipedia.org/wiki/Porcupinefish; http://animals.nationalgeographic.com/animals/fish/pufferfish/
[14] https://en.wikipedia.org/wiki/Shark_tooth
[15] http://www.defenders.org/sharks/basic-facts
[16] https://en.wikipedia.org/wiki/Shark_tooth

Fish and Other Diverse Aquatic Life

Birds: Great Variation Within a Kind

Genesis 1:20 Then God said, "... Let the skies be filled with birds of every kind."

Mountain bluebird (*Sialia currucoides:* top left) North America: "The mountain bluebird (*S. currucoides*) breeds on high-elevation plains from central Alaska to Arizona and New Mexico…"

Great horned owl (*Bubo virginianus:* top middle) "…large owl native to the Americas. It is an extremely adaptable bird with a vast range and is the most widely distributed true owl in the Americas….Adult great horned owls range in length from 43 to 64 cm (17 to 25 in), with an average of 55 cm (22 in), and possess a wingspan of 91 to 153 cm (3 ft 0 in to 5 ft 0 in)…"

Steller's jay (*Cyanocitta stelleri:* top right) "a jay native to western North America, closely related to the blue jay found in the rest of the continent, but with a black head and upper body. It is also known as the long-crested jay, **mountain jay**, and pine jay."

Greater Roadrunner (*Geococcyx californianus:* middle left) "…reach two feet from sturdy bill to white tail tip, with a bushy blue-black crest and mottled plumage that blends well with dusty shrubs. As they run, they hold their lean frames nearly parallel to the ground and rudder with their long tails." https://www.allaboutbirds.org/guide/Greater_Roadrunner/id   The "roadrunner is about 52–62 cm (20–24 in) long, has a 43–61 cm (17–24 in) wingspan…" It can run faster than humans and it can kill rattlesnakes.

Hummingbirds (middle middle) "are New World birds that constitute the family (*Trochilidae*). They are among the smallest of birds, most species measuring in the 7.5–13 cm (3–5 in) range… 338 known species…the average lifespan is probably 3 to 5 years."

Gulls (right, 3rd from top)"often referred to as **seagulls**, are seabirds of the family (*Laridae* in the suborder *Lari*)…Gulls are typically medium to large birds, usually grey or white, often with black markings on the head or wings…Gull species range in size from the little gull, at 120 g (4.2 oz) and 29 cm (11 in), to the great black-backed gull, at 1.75 kg (3.9 lb) and 76 cm (30 in)…"

Rooster (right, 2nd from top), also known as a **cockerel** or **cock**, is a male gallinaceous bird, usually a male chicken (*Gallus gallus*)… A rooster can and will crow at any time of the day."

Ostrich or "**common ostrich** (*Struthio camelus:* bottom left) is either one or two species of large flightless birds native to Africa, the only living member(s) of the genus *Struthio*, which is in the ratite family. …Ostriches usually weigh from 63 to 145 kilograms (139–320 lb), or as much as two adult humans."[17]

Canadian Goose: "*Branta Canadensis* (bottom right) Canada geese nest across inland North America…Both sexes of Canada geese have a black head and neck except for broad white cheek patches extending from the throat to the rear of the eye…7 recognized subspecies…Average length: M 25-45 inches Average weight: M 3-13 lbs., F 3-11 lbs."

---

[17] All references, under the names listed, from Wikipedia, except goose http://www.ducks.org/hunting/waterfowl-id/canada-goose.

Birds Tremendous Variation in Structure and Habits

The Sentinal

Mammals

Genesis 1: 24 Then God said, "Let the earth produce every sort of animal, each producing offspring of the same kind—livestock, small animals that scurry along the ground, and wild animals."

Rock Squirrel (upper left, *Spermophilus variegates),* found in the Southwest US and Oklahoma.[18]

Elk (upper right) "The **elk** or **wapiti** (*Cervus canadensis*) is one of the largest species within the deer family...native to North America and eastern Asia...There are numerous subspecies of elk described, with six from North America and four from Asia...adapted to local environments through minor changes in appearance and behavior" [19] Note: these are two widely separated parts of the earth (and support the idea of transmigration across the Bering Straits at some time in the past, which would be consistent with animal migration post Flood from the Middle East).

Pronghorn (middle left) "The **pronghorn** (*Antilocapra americana*) is a species of artiodactyl mammal indigenous to interior western and central North America. Though not an antelope, it is often known colloquially in North America as the **prong buck**, **pronghorn antelope**, or simply **antelope** because it closely resembles the true antelopes of the Old World..." [20] It is similar to the African Antelope.

Prairie Dog (middle center) "**Prairie dogs** (genus ***Cynomys***) are herbivorous burrowing rodents native to the grasslands of North America. The five species are: black-tailed, white-tailed, Gunnison's, Utah, and Mexican prairie dogs. They are a type of ground squirrel, found in the United States, Canada and Mexico...They feed primarily on grasses and small seeds...live mainly at altitudes ranging from 2,000 to 10,000 ft above sea level... social, prairie dogs live in large colonies or 'towns'... prairie dog families that can span hundreds of acres." [21]

Chimpanzee (middle right) "The **common chimpanzee** (*Pan troglodytes*), also known as the **robust chimpanzee**, is a species of great ape...A chimpanzee's arms are longer than its legs. The male common chimp stands up to 1.2 m (3.9 ft) high and weighs as much as 70 kg (150 lb); the female is somewhat smaller...chimpanzee fossils have been reported from Kenya, indicating that both humans and members of the *Pan* clade were present in the East African Rift Valley during the Middle Pleistocene."[22] Thus, if these comments are true (apart from the assumed age of the Pleistocene) and both human and Pan (chimpanzee) fossils were found in similar strata; this would argue against a common ancestor. Also, some have thought the Chimpanzee by DNA sequencing to be related by progeny to humans. Several scientists have also shown this to not be true.[23] The chimpanzee is simply another mammal with some similar DNA sequences for some similar structure/function relationships determined by the designer/Creator.

Lion (lower left) "The **lion** (*Panthera leo*) is one of the big cats in the genus *Panthera* and a member of the family Felidae...some males exceeding 250 kg (550 lb) in weight...Wild lions currently exist in sub-Saharan Africa and in India...In the late Pleistocene... *Panthera leo spelaea* lived in northern and western Europe and *Panthera leo atrox* lived in the Americas from the Yukon to Peru." [24]

Cat (lower right) "The **domestic cat** (Latin: *Felis catus*) or the **feral cat** (Latin: *Felis silvestris catus*) is a small, typically furry, carnivorous mammal ...part of the genus *Felis*...Members of the genus are found worldwide..." [25]

---

[18] http://www.nhptv.org/natureworks/rocksquirrel.htm

[19] https://en.wikipedia.org/wiki/Elk online 4-24-2016

[20] https://en.wikipedia.org/wiki/Pronghorn

[21] https://en.wikipedia.org/wiki/Prairie_dog

[22] https://en.wikipedia.org/wiki/Common_chimpanzee.

[23]Dr David DeWitt has stated, "40–45 million bases present in humans that are missing from chimps and about the same number present in chimps that are absent from man. These extra DNA nucleotides are called "insertions" or "deletions" because they are thought to have been added to or lost from the original sequence. This puts the total number of DNA differences at about 125 million. However, since the insertions can be more than one nucleotide long, there are about 40 million total separate mutation events that would separate the two species in the evolutionary view... Assuming they did, for the sake of analyzing the argument, then 40 million separate mutation events would have had to take place and become fixed in the population in only 300,000 generations. This is an average of 133 mutations locked into the genome every generation. Locking in such a staggering number of mutations in a relatively small number of generations is a problem referred to as 'Haldane's dilemma.'"   https://answersingenesis.org/genetics/dna-similarities/what-about-the-similarity-between-human-and-chimp-dna/,   and http://creation.com/human-chimp-dna-similarity-re-evaluated.

[24] https://en.wikipedia.org/wiki/Lion Thus, the Lion is another animal that has been found transcontinental, consistent with the Noah Flood Narrative.

[25] https://en.wikipedia.org/wiki/Cat . They are found in SW Asia, Europe, China, Africa and Arabia.

Mammals Diversity of Kinds

Insects and Flowers: A Communion

There is a beauty in the way that insects and flowers interact that may be reminiscent of habits that were present before the corruption of the earth and the life forms on it.

There is a design inherent in insects that is very complex and yet very functional. Barth studied these characteristics: "First Barth covers the insect visual system. **Insects can see colours**: they have trichromatic vision like humans, but most are red blind and ultra-violet sensitive. This is obviously central to understanding flower colours and the presence of visual guideposts for pollinators. Insect visual information processing and pattern recognition distinguish shapes based on figural intensity and figural quality…Barth turns to **insect smell**. Simple experiments show that the olfactory sense of the bee performs very like that of humans…Bees have tens of thousands of pore plates on their antennae, which they can use for 3-D smelling. Flies, beetles, and butterflies use other kinds of noses as well as pore plates — and flies can taste with their feet." [26]

"Species expanded over the land after the Flood diversified, or faded away and new variations appeared. However, the information within the kinds continued on from the original Genesis creations as species adapted and changed. Successful fertilization that follows pollination of a flowering plant produces the growth of seeds and fruit. Although some plants rely on wind (corn, wheat, rice, oats, barley) or water (some aquatic plants) to transfer pollen from one flower to the next, the vast majority (almost 90%) of all plant species need the help of animals for pollination. Pollinators play an important role in maintaining diverse plant communities that provide food for wildlife and ensure pollination for approximately 35 percent of food crops worldwide." [27]

The author in the AIG article cites an example of a unique interaction: Turk's cap lily: "Turk's cap lily (*Lilium superbum*) plants have pendant flowers that hang down, providing no landing pad for heavy beetle or bee pollinators. The unique design however, allows pollination by butterflies. The light-weighted butterfly can grasp the large anthers from below and obtain nectar. This lily is pollinated primarily by swallowtail butterflies..."

Part of her conclusion is: "With a mutualistic relationship, the plant expends less energy in pollen production and instead produces showy flowers, nectar, and/or odors. A flower that attracts specific pollinators on a regular basis has an advantage of wasting less pollen versus flowers that attract promiscuous pollinators. The pollinator gains an advantage of having its own private food source, thereby exerting less energy in competitions between insect species."

Interestingly, there are some plants that release an odor that insects find unacceptable. These plants include the basil which repels flies and mosquitoes; lavender repels moths, fleas, flies, and mosquitoes; lemongrass repels mosquitoes; lemon thyme repels mosquitoes, Rosemary repels mosquitoes and other types of insects. The author has other suggestions as well.[28] Some attributes of flower and insect interaction may reflect original design and others corruption – it is virtually impossible to determine which is the correct assumption.

---

[26] http://dannyreviews.com/h/Insects_Flowers.html This blogger reviews a text titled Insects and Flowers: The Biology of a Partnership Friedrich G. Barth 1991 from Princeton University Press. Unfortunately the book author puts his finding within the evolutionary philosophy.
[27] https://answersingenesis.org/evidence-for-creation/god-created-plant-pollinator-partners/
[28] http://www.mnn.com/your-home/organic-farming-gardening/stories/12-plants-that-repel-unwanted-insects

Insects and Flowers: A Communion

Insects and Flowers: A Communion (continued)

The Beauty of Flowers in the Grand Canyon

Insects: White-Lined Sphinx Moth

White-lined Sphinx *Hyles lineata* (Fabricius,1775) Family: Sphingidae **Subfamily:** Macroglossinae

Range: Central America north through Mexico and the West Indies to most of the United States and southern Canada. Also occurs in Eurasia and Africa. "It has a wingspan of 2 to 3 inches. The moth is sometimes referred to as a *hummingbird moth* because of its similarity to the hummingbird in appearance and flight characteristics… The larva is yellow and black or sometimes lime green and black. Many individuals have a sub-dorsal stripe. The head, pro-thoracic shield, and the anal plate are one color either green or orange with small black dots. The horn varies from either yellow or orange and sometimes has a black tip. Larvae burrow into soil to go into pupal stage, where they remain for 2–3 weeks before they emerge as adults." http://www.butterfliesandmoths.org/species/Hyles-lineata; and https://en.wikipedia.org/wiki/Pupa

Larva stage

"A **pupa** (Latin *pupa* for doll, pl: *pupae* or *pupas*) is the life stage of some insects undergoing transformation. The pupal stage is found only in holometabolous insects, those that undergo a complete metamorphosis, going through four life stages: embryo, larva, pupa and imago"(adult).

Life Cycle Moth: **Egg** to **Larva** (catepillar) to **Pupa** to **Adult** to **Egg** stage

As a biochemist I marvel at the complexity of the life cycle of these kinds of insects. The philosophic assumption of an Intelligent Creator is much more valid than directionless evolution. The processes of **metamorphosis** require the turning on and off of hundreds of genes that code for enzymes that must turn on/off at the precisely correct moments. Mutations in any of the gene protein or regulatory coding regions would cause serious problems. The compounding effects of mutations in any of the stages of metamorphosis would amplify the effects.

For example: Abstract "Metamorphosis is an integrated set of developmental processes controlled by a transcriptional hierarchy that coordinates the action of hundreds of genes." K. White *Science* 10 Dec 1999: Vol. 286, Issue 5447, pp. 2179-2184

For example: Abstract "The actions of steroid hormones on vertebrate and invertebrate nervous systems include alterations in neuronal architecture, regulation of neuronal differentiation, and programmed cell death. In particular, central nervous system (CNS) metamorphosis in insects requires a **precise pattern of exposure** to the steroid molting hormone 20-hydroxyecdysone (ecdysterone)… we examined **Drosophila mutants** of the ecdysterone-regulated locus…the **fusion of right and left brain hemispheres, are deranged in BR-C mutants.**" L.L. Restifo et. al. Dev Biol. 1991 Nov;148(1):174-94

The observation of common design features among widely separated organisms such as the moth and the hummingbird also argues better for an Intelligent Designer and not so called "convergent evolution".

White-Lined Sphinx Moth
Feeding at Night Exquisite Design

The Leaf Curling Spider of Australia

(genus: *Phonognatha*; species: *graeffei*)

Distribution: Eastern Australia. Habitat: Urban areas, forests and woodlands.

Description of the Behaviors and Habitat:

"***Phonognatha graeffei***, referred to as the **Leaf curling spider**, is a common Australian spider found in urban areas as well as woodlands in the North-eastern, Eastern and Southern states. A small member of the Araneidae family, the orb-weavers, it was previously placed in Tetragnathidae." [29]

"They are distinguished by a curled leaf at the web's centre. The species form pairs living together in the same leaf though at opposite ends of their shelter, even before mating at maturity. The female creates a separate curled leaf 'nursery' hung in foliage nearby." [30]

"Leaf-curling Spiders hoist a leaf from the ground, and using silk threads, curl it to form a protective cylinder, silked shut at the top and open at the hub. They then sit in this cylinder with only their legs showing, feeling for the vibrations of a captured insect. The curled leaf protects them from birds and parasitic wasps." [31]

"The body length of the male is 5-6 mm and female 8 to 12 mm. Males look very similar with red-brown legs and body and a cream coloured pattern on their backs. Their bodies are fat and oval shaped with long tapered legs." [32]

This author's comments: It is clear throughout the creation that living organisms have an incredible ability and a type of "understanding" of a way of living in the world that strongly argues for "intelligent design". Evolution does not have an adequate explanation for the development or adaption (if that occurred) of the sophisticated life style of the Leaf Curling Spider. The observations are better placed with the philosophical framework of a Creator and design (albeit a somewhat altered design post fall and corruption of mankind and the creation). That is if the observations are placed within the Christian worldview.

---

[29] Australian Museum, "Leaf Curling Spider", online 11-17-2013.
[30] Ibid.
[31] Wikipedia, *Phonognatha graeffei*, online 11-17-2013.
[32] Ibid.

The Leaf Curling Spider: An Amazing Architect

Spider on web to pick up prey

Spider in the leaf with appendage on the web

Drawing of the Spider in the leaf and the leaf suspended in the web

Wasps

Judges 14:8 mentions "swarms" (Strongs 5712 ants orderly meeting assembly) and "bee" (Strongs 1682 a word meaning orderly motion like a bee).

"Wasps are expert paper makers, capable of turning raw wood into sturdy paper homes. A wasp queen uses her mandibles to scrape bits of wood fiber from fences, logs, or even cardboard. She then breaks the wood fibers down in her mouth, using saliva and water to weaken them. The wasp flies to her chosen nest site with a mouth full of soft paper pulp." [33]

"The nest starts off in the spring with the queen building a petiole (a single stalk from which the nest hangs) and a single hexagonal shaped cell at the end of the petiole, then approx six more cells are formed around the centre one... The queen will lay eggs in each cell as it is being constructed. Once these eggs have hatched out and gone through the developments stages and pupated into adult wasps, these new worker wasps take over nest construction and leave the queen solely to lay eggs and control the nest, this from now on is her primary function!... The wasp colony will die after one season except for the queen who overwinters, emerging in the spring to locate a new nesting site as she will not reuse an old nest." [34]

"While the vast majority of wasps play no role in pollination, a few species can effectively transport pollen and are therefore pollinators of several plant species."[35] The live wasp in the lower left picture is covered with pollen.

The upper photograph shows that wasps are assembled and orderly in their activities.

Fossil wasp (lower right): image reveals little if any change with current wasp structure. It is a living fossil. "*Palaeovespa florissantia*, a fossil wasp (Vespinae) from the Eocene rocks of the Florissant fossil beds of Colorado, c. 34 mya" (Age date by assumed uniformitarian concepts-not accepted by myself). Image from Wikipedia: https://en.wikipedia.org/wiki/Wasp#/media/File:Palaeovespa_florissantia.jpg, listed as public domain.

---

[33] http://insects.about.com/od/antsbeeswasps/qt/how-wasp-nests-are-made.htm
[34] http://www.wasp-removal.com/wasp-nest.php
[35] https://en.wikipedia.org/wiki/Wasp

Wasps:Nesting/feeding Complex Behavior

Dragonflies and Damselflies

"A **dragonfly** is an <u>insect</u> belonging to the order <u>Odonata</u>, <u>suborder</u> **Anisoptera**

(from <u>Greek</u> ανισος *anisos* "uneven" + πτερος *pteros*, "wings", because the <u>hind wing</u> is broader than the <u>forewing</u>). Adult dragonflies are characterized by large <u>multifaceted eyes</u>, two pairs of strong transparent <u>wings</u>, sometimes with colored patches and an elongated body. Dragonflies can be mistaken for the related group, <u>damselflies</u> (Zygoptera), which are similar in structure, though usually lighter in build; however, the wings of most dragonflies are held flat and away from the body, while damselflies hold the wings folded at rest, along or above the abdomen. Dragonflies are agile fliers, while damselflies have a weaker, fluttery flight. Many dragonflies have brilliant iridescent or metallic colours produced by <u>structural coloration</u>, making them conspicuous in flight. An adult dragonfly eye has nearly 24,000 <u>ommatidia</u>." **Dragonfly upper image.**

"**Damselflies** are <u>insects</u> of suborder **Zygoptera** in the order <u>Odonata</u>. They are similar to <u>dragonflies</u>, which constitute the other odonatan suborder, <u>Anisoptera</u>, but are smaller, have slimmer bodies, and most species fold the wings along the body when at rest." **Damselfly lower image.**

Body Part	Dragonfly	Damselfly	Characteristics
Eyes (compound)	Touching at top of head	Separated at top of head	
Thorax/Abdomen	Bulbous thorax with thick abdomen	Bulbous thorax with thin abdomen	Dragonflies larger Damselflies smaller
Wings two pairs	Anterior wings narrower than posterior wings	Anterior and posterior wings about same width	Dragonfly-flies Damselfly-flutters
Pattern of wing veins called Discal cells	Elongated	Triangular	
Legs-three segmented parts	Three pairs of legs	Three pairs of legs	
Terminal Segment of Abdomen (Reproductive)	8-10 total with upper cerci and lower paraprocts	8-10 total with upper cerci and lower paraprocts	
Larvae	Stocky	Slender	

Information from: http://insects.about.com/od/identifyaninsect/a/dragonordamsel.htm; https://en.wikipedia.org/wiki/Damselfly; https://en.wikipedia.org/wiki/Dragonfly

Living Fossils:

Dragonflies have been found in Upper Carboniferous strata (dated by secular reasoning to 325 mya). These were very large with wingspans up to 30 inches. "About 3000 species of Anisoptera are in the world today. Most are tropical, with fewer species in temperate regions."

Damselflies have been found in lower Permian strata (dated by secular reasoning to 250 mya). "All the fossils of that age are of adults, similar in structure to modern damselflies...damselflies are found on every continent except <u>Antarctica</u>." The number of living species are many but is still being classified.

Dragonfly fossil: *Mesuropetala koehleri* Solnhofen Limestone GR (designated Jurassic or 155 mya by secular reasoning). Living fossils argue strongly against evolution and for a short age to the earth.

Dragonflies and Damselflies (Variation in Kind)

Grasshoppers and Crickets

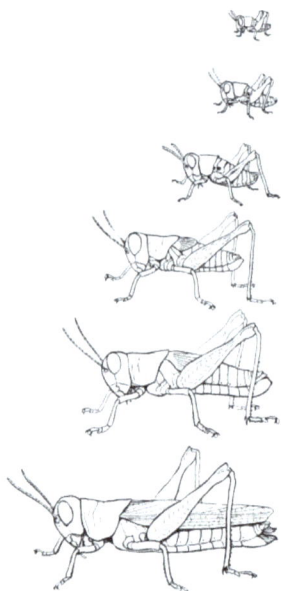

Development of the Grasshopper

From: Grasshopper development by Snodgrass on Wikimedia public domain:
https://commons.wikimedia.org/wiki/File:Snodgrass_Melanoplus_atlanus.png

The difference between Grasshoppers and Crickets

Characteristic	Grasshopper and Locust	Crickets and Katydids
antennae	short	long
auditory organs	on abdomen	On forelegs
stridation	Rub the hind leg against forewing	Rub forewings together
ovipositors	short	Long extended
activity	diurnal	nocturnal
Feeding habits	herbivorous	Predatory, omnivorous, herbivorous

From: http://insects.about.com/od/identifyaninsect/a/grassorcricket.htm

Cricket (fossil) from Brazil in strata assumed to be 125 myo. Crickets and Grasshoppers are "Living Fossils," and are thus support against the evolutionary hypothesis.

Grasshoppers (Variation in Kind)

Praying Mantis

Genesis 7:21 All the living things on earth died—birds, domestic animals, wild animals, **small animals that scurry along the ground**, and all the people.

God made all life and during the Flood all life including insects died if they were not in the Ark. Mantis would have repopulated and developed into the several thousand species post Flood.

"Mantises are an order (**Mantodea**) of insects that contains over 2,400 species and about 430 genera in 15 families. The largest family is the Mantidae ("mantids"). Mantises are distributed worldwide in temperate and tropical habitats. They have triangular heads with bulging eyes supported on flexible necks. Their elongated bodies may or may not have wings, but all Mantodea have forelegs that are greatly enlarged." [36]

"Another advantage for the praying mantis is its coloring. Not only does the mantis' green to grayish-brown offer excellent camouflage in the plant foliage where it prefers to hunt, this color can be somewhat altered by an individual to better match its specific surroundings." [37]

"About 10 native species of praying mantis populate our Southwestern deserts. They range from brownish to tan like our desert soils or to greenish like the desert foliage." [38]

"Adult members of this species range in size from 50–60 mm in body length. There are green, yellow, and brown varieties, with sub-adults and adults tending to have dark transverse bands on the top of the abdomen. The wings of both sexes are mottled or suffused with dark brown or black and the hind wings are purplish. The inner forelegs are orangish, and there are some black spots near the mandibles."[39]

The Praying Mantises in the picture are probably *Stagmomantis californica*, common name California mantis, is a species of praying mantis in the genus *Stagmomantis* native to the Western United States. (See reference 40.)

Question: What was the habitat and behavior of the Praying Mantis before the Fall? It is an aggressive hunter, either by ambush or stalking it pray-other insects and eats them alive. The female sometimes eats the male mate after mating.[40] These current characteristics do not seem to be what they would have had prior to the Fall. Science cannot answer the question. All it can do is observe the current behavior. Have they mutated from their original form? Gene mutational load is degrading every life form. Maybe mantises were made to mulch leaves initially.

---

[36] Wikipedia Praying Mantis.
[37] http://aggie-horticulture.tamu.edu/galveston/beneficials/beneficial-20_mantid_praying_mantis.htm
[38] http://www.desertusa.com/insects/praying-mantis.html#ixzz46Ykpeahe
[39] https://en.wikipedia.org/wiki/Stagmomantis_californica
[40] http://www.wildlife.state.nm.us/download/education/conservation/wildlife-notes/insects-spiders/praying-mantis.pdf

Praying Mantis (Variation in Kind/Size)

Trees: Bristlecone Pine Trees

Psalm 119:130 All your words are true; all your righteous laws are eternal.

"A bristlecone pine can refer to one of three species of pine trees (family Pinaceae, genus Pinus, subsection Balfouriannae). All three species are long-lived and highly resistant to harsh weather and bad soils. One of the three species, Pinus longaeva, is among the longest-lived life forms on Earth. The oldest Pinus longaeva is more than 5,000 years old, making it the oldest known individual of any species."[41]

These pines grow "high in the White Mountains in Inyo County in eastern California. The Great Basin Bristlecone Pine (Pinus longaeva) trees grow between 9,800 and 1,000 feet (3,00-3,400 m) above sea level…(and grow) on dolomitic soils. The trees grow in soils that are shallow lithosols, usually derived from dolomite and sometimes limestone, and occasionally sandstone or quartzite soils. Dolomite soils are alkaline, high in calcium and magnesium, and low in phosphorus. Those factors tend to exclude other plant species, allowing bristlecones to thrive. Because of cold temperatures, dry soils, high winds, and short growing seasons, the trees grow very slowly. Even the tree's needles, which grow in bunches of five, can remain on the tree for forty years, which gives the tree's terminal branches the unique appearance of a long bottle brush."[42]

To date trees the methods are used below. From this the oldest tree in the forest was calculated: Five types of ages are recognized in the database: XD: cross-dated (overlap with other trees), RC: ring counted, EX: extrapolations (usually based on ring measurements), HI: historic record, C14: radiocarbon dated wood samples from a tree (added 2007). The result: Pinus longaeva   date 5062 y/o by the XD method, found White Mountains, CA.[43]

However, it has been shown that multiple growth rings per year can occur in the BCP. "Lammerts, a creationist, induced multiple ring growth in sapling BCPs by simply simulating a two week drought…An expert in the genus Pinus didn't seem to have any problem believing that White Mountain BCPs grew multiple rings per year. In his book, The Genus Pinus, Mirov states, 'Apparently a semblance of annual rings is formed after every rather infrequent cloudburst.'" [44] Woodmorpape disagreed with this claim, "The 8,000-year-long BCP chronology appears to be correctly cross-matched, and there is no evidence that bristlecone pines can put on more than one ring per year…(but may be explained by) existence of migrating ring-disturbing events." [45]   Thus, an exact age for the trees probably cannot be determined but it fits within a young earth.

[41] https:en.wikipedia.org/wiki/Bristlecone_pine.
[42] https://en.wikipedi.org/wiki/Ancient_Bristlecone_Pine_Forest.
[43] http://www.rmtrr.org/oldlist.htm
[44] http://creation.com/evidence-for-multiple-ring-growth-per-year-in-bristlecone-pines (written 2006)
[45] https://answersingenesis.org/age-of-the-earth/biblical-chronology-and-8000-year-bristlecone-pine-chronology/ (written 2009)

Bristlecone Pine One of the Oldest Living Life Forms

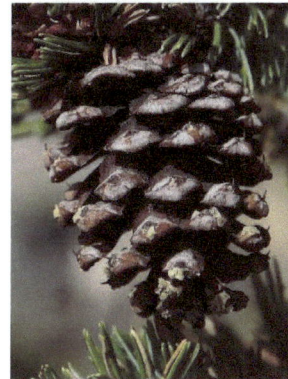

Sequoia Pine Trees

Psalm 104:1,16 Let all that I am praise the LORD. O LORD my God, how great you are! You are robed with honor and majesty. … The trees of the LORD are well cared for— the cedars of Lebanon that **he planted.** (Author's note: God planted the trees.)

"*Sequoiadendron giganteum* (giant sequoia, giant redwood, Sierra redwood, Sierran redwood, or Wellingtonia) is the sole living species in the genus *Sequoiadendron*, and one of three species of coniferous trees known as redwoods,.. It is named after Sequoyah (1767–1843), the inventor of the Cherokee syllabary…The natural distribution of giant sequoias is restricted to a limited area of the western Sierra Nevada, California. They occur in scattered groves, with a total of 68 groves (see list of sequoia groves for a full inventory), comprising a total area of only 144.16 km^2 (35,620 acres)… The natural distribution of giant sequoias is restricted to a limited area of the western Sierra Nevada, California. They occur in scattered groves, with a total of 68 groves (see list of sequoia groves for a full inventory), comprising a total area of only 144.16 km^2 (35,620 acres)… Wood from mature giant sequoias is highly resistant to decay, but due to being fibrous and brittle, it is generally unsuitable for construction. " [46]

"Giant sequoias can grow to be about 30 feet (9 meters) in diameter and more than 250 feet (76 meters) tall. The biggest of these behemoths is General Sherman, a giant sequoia in Sequoia National Park. General Sherman stands 275 feet (84 meters) tall, has a 102-foot (31 meters) circumference, and weighs an incredible 2.7 million pounds (1.2 million kilograms). Giant sequoias can live to 3,000 years, with the oldest on record living more than 3,500 years." [47]

The General Sherman Tree is the greatest in mass in the park. Height 275 ft or 84 m; girth at ground 103 ft or 31 m; volume 52,508 cubic ft or 1,487 cubic m. (see Wikipedia article)

Sequoias are burn resistant. The burn in the base of this tree has begun to close, and the tree remains viable even after a significant burn.

---

[46] https://en.wikipedia.org/wiki/Sequoiadendron_giganteum
[47] http://www.livescience.com/39461-sequoias-redwood-trees.html

Sequoia Pine Trees One of the Largest Living Life Forms on Earth

Mountains & Valleys: Canyon de Chelly

Genesis 7:19 Finally, the water covered even the highest mountains on the earth, **20** rising more than twenty-two feet above the highest peaks.

A report in 1916 described the "De Chelly sandstone. Massive, very cross-bedded red or brown sandstone, 0-585 feet thick, uncomformably underlying Shinarump conglomerate and overlying Moenkopi formation in Navajo country, Age is Permian (?)."
Online http://ngmdb.usgs.gov/Geoles/UnitRefs/DeChelly_7852.html Article title USGS Water-Supply Paper 380, 1916.

"A 1975 study by scientists Freeman and Visher (*Journal of Sedimentary Petrology*, 45:3:651-668) provides some important insights as to the origin of the Navajo Sandstone. The investigators pointed out that underwater sand dunes are known to accumulate on portions of the sea floor swept by strong currents--for example, beneath the North Sea. Superficially they look a lot like desert (windblown) sand dunes, but careful analysis of their grain size distribution reveals major differences. It turns out that disaggregated sands from the Navajo Sandstone match very well with modern submarine dunes, and very poorly with desert dunes." http://www.icr.org/article/marketing-navajo-sandstone/

It is probable that the De Chelly Sandstone represents water laden sand dunes as well. This would require fast moving waters in massive amounts. The Shinarump conglomerate also appears to have been deposited in a similar fashion. It seems probable that massive rapid erosion would have occurred post Flood to form the pedicles seen in the photos.

photo 1871

http://creation.com/defining-the-flood-post-flood-boundary-in-sedimentary-rocks
"The Shinarump Conglomerate outcrops over 260,000 km^2 on the Colorado Plateau and is only about 15 m thick. The formation consists of sand and rounded pebbles. It is also lithified. Thus, from the first three criteria presented in tables 1 and 3, the deposit is likely from the Flood. It is dated as Mesozoic in the geological column." He lists these criteria: Tall erosional remnants, planation surfaces and pediments, long transported cobbles and boulders, thin horizontally widespread sediments or sedimentary rock, large volumes of sediment or sedimentary rock, and lithified sediments.

Canyon De Chelly

Grand Canyon's Three Sets of Rocks

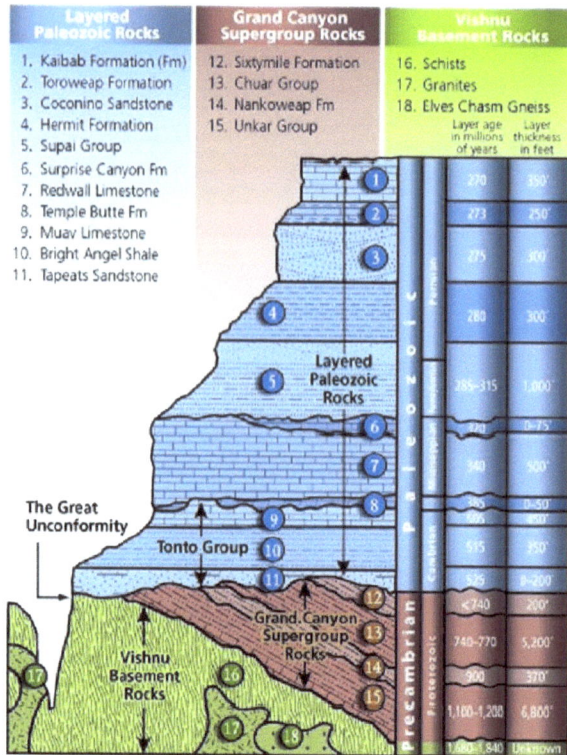

Layered Paleozoic Rocks	Grand Canyon Supergroup Rocks	Vishnu Basement Rocks
1. Kaibab Formation (Fm) 2. Toroweap Formation 3. Coconino Sandstone 4. Hermit Formation 5. Supai Group 6. Surprise Canyon Fm 7. Redwall Limestone 8. Temple Butte Fm 9. Muav Limestone 10. Bright Angel Shale 11. Tapeats Sandstone	12. Sixtymile Formation 13. Chuar Group 14. Nankoweap Fm 15. Unkar Group	16. Schists 17. Granites 18. Elves Chasm Gneiss

< Tapeats Sandstone stratified rock

< Vishnu Basement Rock crystalline metamorphic

The Great Uncomformity

The Great Unconformity: The Tapeats Sandstone (layered strata) dated 525 myo (per secular sources) overlies the Vishnu crytalline metamorphic rock dated 1,700 myo. A complete lack of a widespread strata for ONE BILLION YEARS. **This vast gap of widespread strata can be explained more reasonable by a massive Flood rather than slow accumulation under uniformitarrian processes.** Figure from NPS public domain and photograph by JGL. Dates for rock units from NPS and Wikipedia.

Grand Canyon

Upper

Middle

Lower

Mountain Buttes and Rims

(Support for Catastrophic Reconstruction of the Earth)

Buttes: a "**butte** is an isolated hill with steep, often vertical sides and a small, relatively flat top; buttes are smaller than mesas, plateaus, and table landforms. The word butte comes from a French word meaning "small hill"; its use is prevalent in the Western United States, including the southwest where "mesa" is also used for the larger landform. Because of their distinctive shapes, buttes are frequently landmarks in plains and mountainous areas. In differentiating mesas and buttes, geographers use the rule of thumb that a mesa has a top that is wider than its height, while a butte has a top that is narrower than its height." [48]

Example of a significant butte: "Red Butte is composed of flat-lying shale of the Moenkopi Formation, overlain by Shinarump Conglomerate of the Chinle Formation. Continuous exposures of these two formations are not found for tens of miles around, yet they occur here. These strata sit on a foundation of flat-lying and resistant Kaibab Limestone, the rim rock for most of Grand Canyon and surface of the Coconino Plateau. A basalt (lava) flow tops the butte, protecting the softer layers below from erosion." These strata were once "1,000 feet higher than the present Coconino Plateau! Strata of the Moenkopi, Chinle, and perhaps other formations were stripped away by erosion. Red Butte stands as the most prominent vestige of this once continuous layer…" **The Flood provides a reasonable model for the massive erosion that must have occurred and "Red Butte is a tiny remnant from this vast erosion."**[49]

Mogollon Rim: "is a topographical and geological feature cutting across the U.S. state of Arizona. It extends approximately 200 miles (320 km), starting in northern Yavapai County and running eastward, ending near the border with New Mexico. It forms the southern edge of the Colorado Plateau in Arizona… characterized by high cliffs of limestone and sandstone, namely the Kaibab Limestone and Coconino Sandstone cliffs." [50]

"The Pacific Plate and the North American Continental Plate tectonics have wrinkled and stretched Arizona's geologic crust, forming the states mountain ranges and valleys, ridges and depressions, and mineral outcroppings. The Mogollon Rim is an extended and uniform geologic monocline or fold consequent to the region's plate tectonics…The fold has eroded in such a way as to create a three hundred-mile-long escarpment that has retreated north-northeastward in an impressive uniformity…Along this rim, evidence of geologically recent volcanic activity is plentiful and dominates the landscape for hundreds of miles." [51] **The buckling and bending of vast areas of strata are consistent with post-Flood deformation of soft layers of earth.**

Dr. Tas Walker, a geologist, has commented (regarding the Grand Canyon), "Yet, the evidence indicates that the sediments were soft and unconsolidated when they bent. Instead of fracturing like the basement did, the entire layer thinned as it bent." [52]

---

[48] https://en.wikipedia.org/wiki/Butte
[49] https://www.icr.org/article/3755/
[50] https://en.wikipedia.org/wiki/Mogollon_Rim
[51] http://jsw.library.arizona.edu/3403/geog.html
[52] http://creation.com/grand-canyon-strata-show-geologic-time-is-imaginary

Mountain Buttes and Rims

A butte near Chaco Canyon NM

Red Butte-near the South Rim of the Grand Canyon

Profile of the Grand Canyon

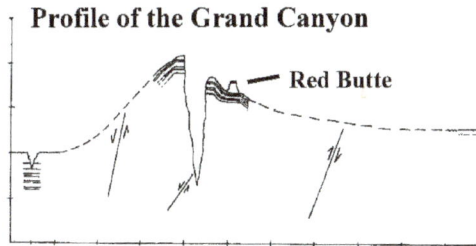

Red Butte

Mogollon Rim-in winter

Sandia Mountains

(Fossils in multiple Conformed layers of Limestone on top, a Large Uncomformity between Carboniferous Limestone and Granite, and Massive Uplift all consistent with a Large Catastrophic Flood Deposition and Post Deposit Deformation)

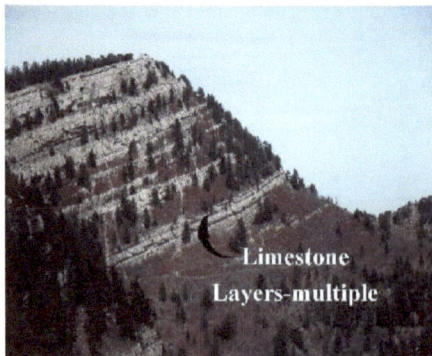

Limestone
Granite
Sandia Mountains Elevation 10,679 ft
(Diagram from USGS and NPS with permit)
Limestone Layers-multiple
Sandstone/Cretaceous Limestone
Unconformity
Granite
Fossil Crinoids Carboniferous Layer Top Sandia Mountains

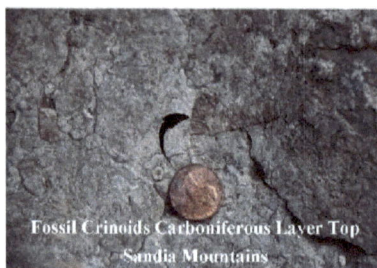

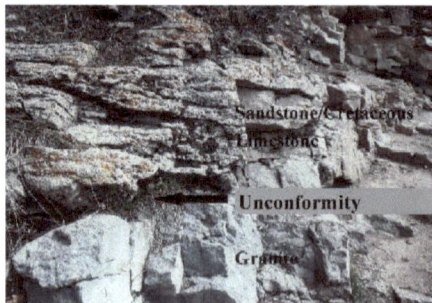

Evidence for a Massive Flood and Post-Flood Upheaval:

1) Stratified layers of rock consistent with formation under water in that they have fossil forms consistent with previously live organisms-all jammed together. The layers are on top of the Sandia Mountains, elevation 10,679 feet above sea level. They are composed of limestone. It is considered to be 300 myo by secular reasoning.

2) Below is granite crystalline rock. It is considered to be 1,500 myo by secular reasoning. Thus, there is a gap of ONE BILLION YEARS . See photo to see the knife edge conformity between these formations. It is extremely unlikely to have not had some sedimentation occuring, and if erosion had occured during that time it would have had to be rapid and massive. Thus, the observations fit better with the Noah Flood Account. Dates/strata taken from Wikipedia on the Sandia Mountains geology.

It should be also be noted: the gap of a supposed one and one half billion years in the Grand Canyon is between the Tapeats Sandstone and granite below, but with Cretaceous Limestone above the granite in the Sandias. These strata are of different composition and supposed ages (525 vs 300 myo). In both areas, separated by 394 miles, the concept of a massive ebbing and flowing of differing flood strata seems more plausible.

The Rocky Mountains With Sandia Mountains

Yosemite

"The major, almost exclusive, rock type in some areas on the earth's surface, such as in the Yosemite National Park, is granite. Huge masses of many adjoining granite bodies outcrop on a grand scale throughout that area…"[53]

"Granites constitute a major portion of the continental crust. They outcrop over many areas of the earth's surface as discrete bodies called plutons, ranging in size from 10 km^2 to thousands of km^2. The granite magmas are believed to be sourced from great depths in the lower to mid levels of the continental crust, but the plutons crystallize in the upper crust, typically at depths of 1–5 km…Granites are composed of several major minerals (quartz, K-feldspar, plagioclase, biotite, & hornblende), with minor constituents such as zircon (zirconium silicate). Tiny zircon grains (1–5 microns in diameter) are often found encased within large flakes (1–5 mm in diameter) of ubiquitous biotite. The zircon grains usually carry trace amounts of ^{238}U, whose radioactive decay has provided a means by which it is claimed the ages of granites can be measured. Nevertheless, as the ^{238}U in the zircon grains decays to ^{206}Pb, it leaves physical evidence of that decay in the form of radiohalos, spherical zones of discoloration around these zircon grains (the radiocenters). Radiohalos are, in fact, the damage left by the emission of alpha (a) during the ^{238}U decay process."

"Polonium radiohalos found in biotite flakes of granites in Yosemite National Park place severe time constraints on the formation and cooling of the granite plutons due to the short half-lives of the polonium isotopes. The biotite flakes must have formed and cooled below 150°C before the polonium supply was exhausted and the radiohalos could be preserved, so the U decay had to be grossly accelerated and the formation of the plutons had to be within 6–10 days."[54]

"The timescale for the generation of granitic magmas and their subsequent intrusion, crystallization, and cooling as plutons is no longer incompatible with the biblical time frames of the global, year-long Flood cataclysm and of 6,000–7,000 years for earth history… Rapid segregation, ascent, and emplacement now understood to only take days via dikes would have been aided by the tectonic "squeezing" and "pumping" during the catastrophic plate tectonics driving the global Genesis Flood cataclysm… crystallization and cooling would be even more easily facilitated by hydrothermal convective circulation with meteoric waters in the host rocks. The growth of large crystals from magmas within hours has now been experimentally determined…"[55]

The predominance of granite and its likely rapid formation within Yosemite National Park area is consistent with a catastrophic formation which occurred during and after the Flood.

[53] https://answersingenesis.org/geology/catastrophism/catastrophic-granite-formation/
[54] https://answersingenesis.org/geology/radiometric-dating/polonium-radiohalos-tuolumne-intrusive-suite-yosemite-california/
[55] https://answersingenesis.org/geology/catastrophism/catastrophic-granite-formation/

Yosemite Falls California

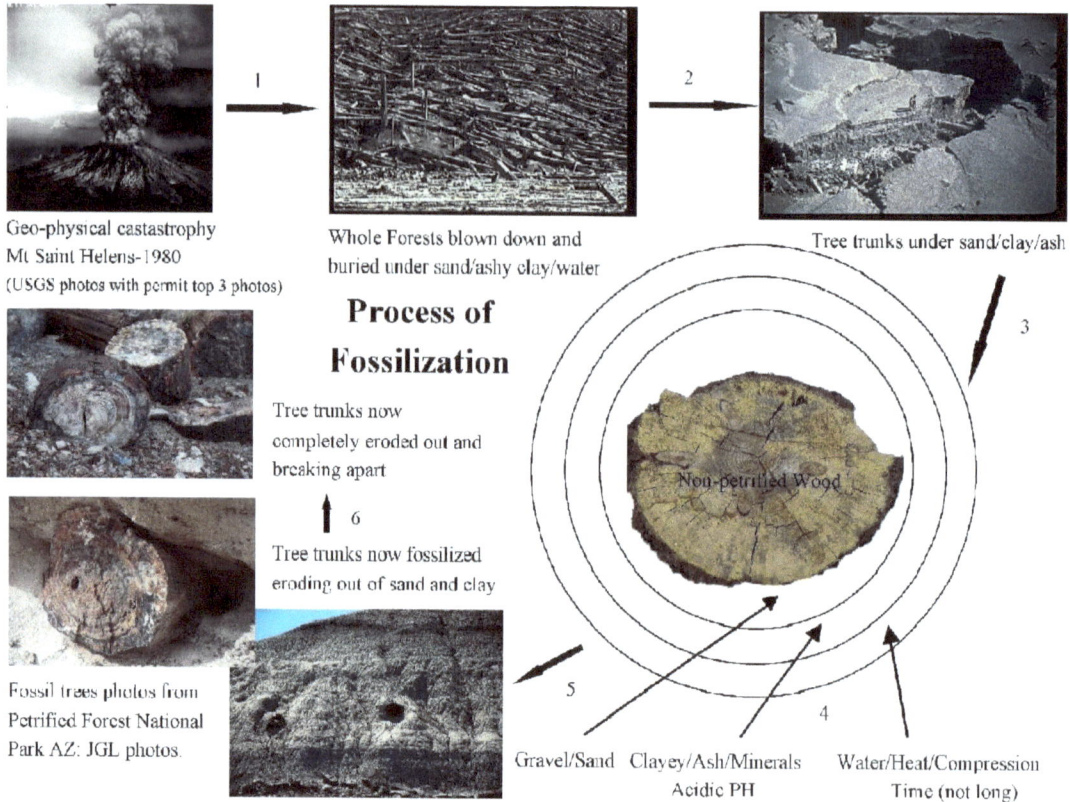

Geo-physical castastrophy
Mt Saint Helens-1980
(USGS photos with permit top 3 photos)

Whole Forests blown down and
buried under sand/ashy clay/water

Tree trunks under sand/clay/ash

Process of Fossilization

Tree trunks now
completely eroded out and
breaking apart

Tree trunks now fossilized
eroding out of sand and clay

Non-petrified Wood

Fossil trees photos from
Petrified Forest National
Park AZ: JGL photos.

Gravel/Sand   Clayey/Ash/Minerals   Water/Heat/Compression
                      Acidic PH   Time (not long)

Painted Desert figure legend: 1) large logs aligned parallel to each other indicating considerable watery flow at the time of deposition and not a meandering stream; **2)** many large trees with fossilized root bulbs with the root ends torn off in antiquity; **3)** massive layers of matted root material; **4)** bark fossilized while in the process of pealing of from the cambrium layer of the tree; **5)** fossil tree remains with no bark layer remaining, similar to what was seen at Mt St. Helens in 1980; **6)** fossil logs lying parallel in a layer of clay and ashe most consistent with catastrophic burial, **7)** fossil branch inserts consistent with removal in antiquity; **8/9)** logs encased with soil that has hardened into a cement. It was probably rich in lime and and low ph as would be present with massive flooding around a volcano.**10)** volcanic capstone over the clayey layers which probably trapped in the moisture, heat, low ph, minerals, silicates, and anoxic environment necessary for fossilization to occur.

Painted Desert

Painted Desert Petrified Forest Evidence for a Catastrophy

Painted Desert Arizona

The Beauty of the Creation Even in the Corruption of it

Blue -copper
Orange-iron
Pink-iron
White-quartz

Grey-manganese
Black-carbon or
manganese

Yellow-iron

Clouds

Genesis 9:11 Yes, I am confirming my covenant with you. Never again will floodwaters kill all living creatures; never again will a flood destroy the earth." **12** Then God said, "**I am giving you a sign of my covenant with you and with all living creatures, for all generations to come. 13 I have placed my rainbow in the clouds. It is the sign of my covenant with you and with all the earth. 14 When I send clouds over the earth, the rainbow will appear in the clouds, 15 and I will remember my covenant** with you and with all living creatures. Never again will the floodwaters destroy all life.

Psalm 104:1 Let all that I am praise the LORD . O LORD my God, how great you are! You are robed with honor and majesty. **2** You are dressed in a robe of light. **You stretch out the starry curtain of the heavens; 3 you lay out the rafters of your home in the rain clouds**. You make the **clouds your chariot**; you ride upon the wings of the wind. **4**The winds are your messengers; flames of fire are your servants. **5** You **placed the world on its foundation** so it would never be moved.

Psalm 108:1 My heart is confident in you, O God; no wonder I can sing your praises with all my heart! **2** Wake up, lyre and harp! I will wake the dawn with my song. **3** I will thank you, LORD, among all the people. I will sing your praises among the nations. **4 For your unfailing love is higher than the heavens. Your faithfulness reaches to the clouds**. **5** Be exalted, O God, above the highest heavens. May your glory shine over all the earth.

Daniel 7:13 As my vision continued that night, I saw **someone like a son of man coming with the clouds of heaven. He approached the Ancient One** and was led into his presence. **14** He was given authority, honor, and sovereignty over all the nations of the world, so that people of every race and nation and language would obey him. His rule is eternal—it will never end. His kingdom will never be destroyed.

Matthew 24:29 "Immediately after the anguish of those days, the sun will be darkened, the moon will give no light, the stars will fall from the sky, and the powers in the heavens will be shaken. **30** And then at last, the sign that the **Son of Man is coming will appear in the heavens**, and there will be deep mourning among all the peoples of the earth. And they will see the **Son of Man coming on the clouds of heaven with power and great glory**. **31** And he will send out his angels with the mighty blast of a trumpet, and they will **gather his chosen ones from all over the world** —from the farthest ends of the earth and heaven.

To God Be The Glory-Come Lord Jesus Christ

Clouds of the Southwest US

Geometric Design

"Geometric analysis is, by definition, the application of methods from analysis (in particular, from nonlinear PDE) to study both local and global geometry, although it turns out that in addition to analysis, methods from algebraic geometry and representation theory are also very powerful and important. Modern geometry is now a vast subject, for instance extending beyond its traditional roots in real and complex surfaces to arithmetic surfaces (as discussed earlier on this blog), and also interacting very fruitfully (and bi-directionally) with modern physics such as general relativity and string theory…With this viewpoint, the only co-ordinate changes in a geometry which one should permit are those which preserve some specific algebraic structure in that geometry (e.g. complex structure, affine structure, conformal structure, projective structure, symplectic structure, or foliated structure). For instance, on complex manifolds, one should only consider co-ordinate changes which are holomorphic."[56]

publicdomainvectors.org

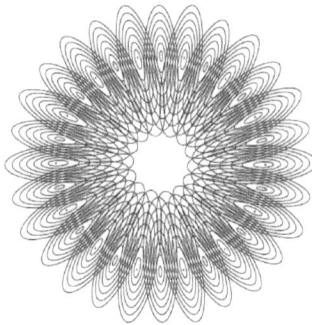

Drawing of a 3 D object   Drawing of a 2 D object[57]   Drawing of Solar System-Kepler 1595[58]

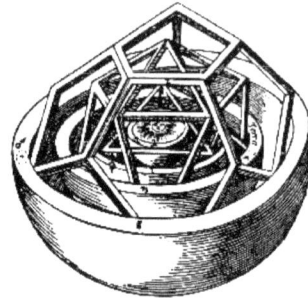

Tragically some use the framework of evolution to project geometric designs. Their comments take on the form of religious thought. [59,60] Yet, it is indeed still more reasonable to believe in a Creator outside of the physical creation who thought and spoke all of it into being. However, no matter which view one takes: 1) the ability of matter to self organize, or 2) an Intelligent Creator who created matter; it remains a religious view which science cannot referee on. Science can only observe the phenomenon. Note: Kepler was a devout Christian.

---

[56] terrytao.wordpress.com/2007/05/15/distinguished-lecture-series-i-shing-tung-yau-what-is-a-geometric-tructure/
[57] http://publicdomainvectors.org/en/free-geometric-design-clip-art online 6-28-16.
[58] https://en.wikipedia.org/wiki/Johannes_Kepler
[59] *The evolution of geometric structures on 3-manifolds* by C McMullin in 2010: "In contrast to the case of surfaces, which are ordered by genus, the world 3 of 3-manifolds resembles an evolutionary tree, with phyla and species whose intricate variations admit, at best, a partial ordering by various measures of complexity." ww.math.harvard.edu/~ctm/papers/home/text/papers/evo/evo.pdf
[60] http://creation.com/evolution-religious: 'The biggest thing going for Darwinism was that it finally broke the tyranny in which Christianity had held the minds of men for so many centuries'—Sir Fred Hoyle (1915–2001) and Prof. Chandra Wickramasinghe (b. 1939), in 1983. Tragically, many of mankind gave up God for Religious Atheism.

Geometric Structures

Geometric structures-how did they come about? Science can not answer this question. It can observe the process of development, look at gene sequences and manipulate them; but then it is still unanswered: how did such complex structures come about? Elimination over great periods of time where the seed dispersal of this plant was more succesful than others? Only a biased view can accept that answer. For myself the concept of an Intelligent Creator makes more sense. Even man can create such structures through thought and experimentation-but then the Bible says that man is made in God's Image. Yet, we are NOT God but His imprint is on humans. **Gen. 1: 27 So God created man in his own image, in the image of God created he him; male and female created he them. KJV**
The flower is a *Tragopogon dubius* Scop.– yellow salsify (a transplant from Central Europe to the US) Wikipedia.

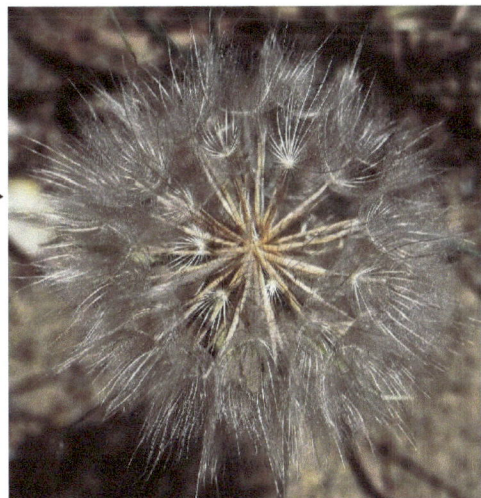

Conclusion

In the preceding pages it was demonstrated that all of life forms: plants, insects, reptile/amphibians, mammals and man have complex bodily and social structures. These aspects of life are <u>not</u> amenable to simple supposed evolutionary progressions. And so-called "living fossils" argue strongly against evolution. Yet, the commonality of design and function, seen in wide varieties of life forms and their habits, argues more reasonably with the intelligent design of a Creator.

Science can not differentiate between life having been created or evolved. These events occurred before the process of human observation, and life forms are not evolving today nor are they being created. One must choose which religio-philosophical system, an atheistic or Creator source, to accept for the beginning and ending of themselves and all other life forms.[61, 62]

Yet even in the beauty and complexity of life forms there is a general trend towards degradation. These life forms are in a process of progressive dying. This argues against evolution, but an explanation needs to be sought regarding why a Creator would allow His creation to degrade. The Biblical scriptures give the explanation:

Romans 5:12 When Adam sinned, sin entered the world. Adam's sin brought death, so death spread to everyone, for everyone sinned. [63]

And the impact of man's sin has spread throughout the entire physical earth as seen in:

Romans 8:20 Against its will, all creation was subjected to God's curse. But with eager hope, **21** the creation looks forward to the day when it will join God's children in glorious freedom from death and decay. **22** For we know that all creation has been groaning as in the pains of childbirth right up to the present time. **23** And we believers also groan, even though we have the Holy Spirit within us as a foretaste of future glory, for we long for our bodies to be released from sin and suffering. We, too, wait with eager hope for the day when God will give us our full rights as his adopted children, including the new bodies he has promised us. **24** We were given this hope when we were saved. (If we already have something, we don't need to hope for it. **25** But if we look forward to something we don't yet have, we must wait patiently and confidently.)

See the next page for an explanation of what it means to become a Christian.

---

[61] See http://creation.com/religion-science-philosophy-interface-noah-flood for a further explanation of these ideas.
[62] www.DefendingtheChristianFaith.org.
[63] Sin is to miss the mark or the calling of God for a person, which includes the acknowledgment that each living human being was born a sinner and apart from God. But, through the perfect life and death of Jesus Christ, a person can be forgiven their sin and regain fellowship with God if they choose to accept Christ's sacrifice for them. See The Creator's Plan For You-next page.

THE CREATOR'S PLAN FOR YOU

The Creator's Plan for You

Ancient writings and all cultures of the world teach about the Creator, a worldwide flood which destroyed the surface of the earth because of the sins of man, and the need of a blood sacrifice to atone for these sins to be at peace with Almighty God.

The sacred scriptures of the Bible teach that as a man Jesus Christ came from God, to die as the blood payment for all men's sins, and that whoever accepted His sacrifice for their sins would be forgiven of them. As God, Christ Jesus could then give them new life, by recreating the hearts of those forgiven. They could then live eternally with God now and after death.

Would you like to do this? If so, the AACTS steps below are suggested:

1) The book of Romans 3:23 says, "For all have sinned (disobeyed) and fall short of the glory of God." Admit that you have sinned.

2) Romans 6:23 states, "For the wages of sin is death, but the free gift of God is eternal life in Christ Jesus our Lord." Acknowledge sin is leading you to death (physically, emotionally, spiritually).

3) Romans 10:9-10 says, "That if you confess with your mouth Jesus as Lord, and believe in your heart that God raised Him from the dead, you shall be saved; for with the heart man believes resulting in righteousness (right standing with God) and with the mouth he confesses resulting in salvation (freed forever from the punishment of sin)." If you Confess the Teachings of the Bible, that Jesus is Lord and He died for your sins, you will experience Salvation.

4) So AACTS now! And get involved in a local church that teaches the Bible.

*Quotations from the NAS Bible used with permission. Deluge 2000

55

About the Author

Dr. John G. Leslie received a PhD on September 7th 2012 in the field of Archaeology and Biblical History from Trinity Southwest University (TSWU), Albuquerque, NM. He presently taken part in the annual dig of a biblical site in the Jordan Valley. There he has been studying the human and animal bone artifacts. His association with TSWU has been since 2004.

As well, Dr Leslie has been practicing medicine in a medically underserved area of the Southwest United States for 20 years. He made a commitment to God to do this after he returned to medical school in his mid-thirties. The training for an MD was at Oral Roberts University, with graduation in 1989. He then went to the University of Oklahoma Tulsa Branch to complete dual residencies in both Internal Medicine and Pediatrics in 1993, and subsequently became board certified in both fields.

Prior to going to medical school Dr Leslie completed a PhD in Experimental Pathology in 1980 from the University of Utah. He worked with one of the world's leading specialists studying the structure and metabolism of Elastin, one of the key structural proteins of the body. After completing this degree he worked at Monash University in Melbourne Australia as a post-doctoral researcher for 4 years till returning to medical school. His undergraduate BS degree was from the American University in Washington, DC in 1973.

From: http://creationwiki.org/John_Leslie

Dr Leslie committed his life to Jesus Christ, and experienced being "born again" late 1974. Several people were key to this happening in his life-most significant was his Godly mother Doris Gregory Leslie. As well, he and his wife Barbara have served God in various ways including Pro-life causes during their married life of 35 years. They have three grown children serving God.

To God Be The Glory

The Author and his wife

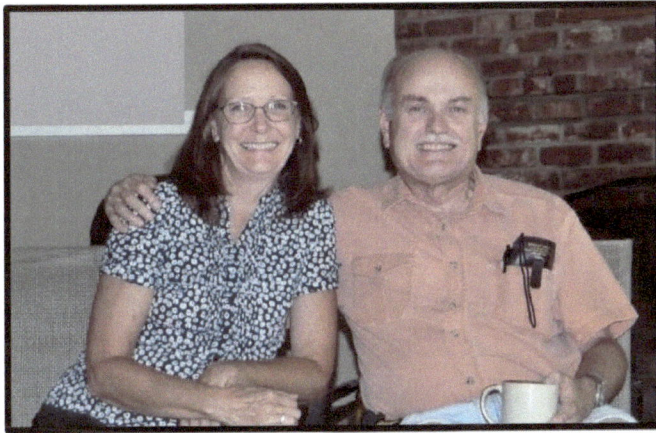

For information on a variety of issues see:
www.DefendingtheChristianFaith.org

www.ingramcontent.com/pod-product-compliance
Lightning Source LLC
Chambersburg PA
CBHW060847270326
41934CB00002B/31